THE QUILTING BIBLE

Emma Stitchwood

TABLE OF CONTENTS

INTRODUCTION TO QUILTING

Definition

Quilting is a process of stitching multiple layers of fabric together. It requires you to use at least three layers of fabric; the upper and lower cloth layers with a third layer of padding (wadding) in between. All these layers are stitched together via threads to make a quilt. You must have seen how quilts are used as bed covers. You can do quilting either manually by thread and needle or use a sewing machine to do so!

Why Quilting? Benefits and Enjoyment

Quilting has a sacred purpose and meaning. They save you from a cold environment and keep you warm. The one who quilts the fabric stitches it with love and affection to show appreciation to their dear ones. Not only do you learn self-expression by quilting but they also connect you with deep lessons of life. Such as the quilters of Gee's Bend (a revolutionary journey of American African females to gain economic independence).

Hence, tracing from the history, quilting helps you feel accomplished. In the beginning, this task can be challenging. However, once you complete a project successfully, the achievement is totally worth the effort!

Here's why you may start quilting!

1. Enhanced Coordination Skills

Are you afraid that your reflexes are getting slower? Would you like a perfect way to fasten up your motor and coordination skills? If so, you'd be glad to learn that quilting can improve your hand movements and coordination. It requires precise attention and detailing. Consequently, it helps you exercise your hand-eye movement and fine motor skills. Quilting is highly recommended for older adults!

2. Sense of accomplishment

Many researches show that as you age, your ability to perform certain tasks declines. Therefore, the motivation and will to accomplish something also deters. In this condition, quilting can be a great way to make your life enthusiastic and committed to goals.

It also helps you fight depression. You can also share your pride with family and friends. There are many quilting communities online where beginners share their art to get feedback from fellows!

3. Better Heart Health

This needlecraft hobby can help your body stay happy, calm, and stress-free. Quilting works as therapy and can counteract by lowering your heart rate and blood pressure.

4. Flexibility and Activity

If you want to get rid of your lousy couch and TV routine, quilting can help you there. Quilting involves many sensory and physical movements that are necessary for a healthy body. It won't be anywhere near Olympic activity, but the procedure can retain body flexibility.

Quilting involves stretching the fabric, cutting fabric pieces, and working on a sewing machine or manually. These activities can make you stretch your hands and muscles effectively.

5. Improved Sleep

Quilting impacts your body and mind positively. It soothes your mind by helping you with a sense of direction and purpose. Hence, as you quilt, the muscles are constantly working. So, it results in a restful and sound sleep.

6. High Self-esteem

Completing a quilting piece can boost your mood and give you a sense of pride. It can be incredibly satisfying when you successfully show your work to others.

Quilting has many health and wellness benefits. Once, you learn the basics, there's much more fun to this habit such as textures, colours, designs, and fabrics. Stay tuned to learn more!

Essential Fabrics

It can be a straining task to pick the right fabric for quilting. It is a whole jungle of different patterns, materials, weights, and designs. Hence, as a beginner, you first need to know what fabrics are essential to start!

1. Quilter's Weight Cotton

It is the most common and famous fabric of the quilting world. This fabric is quite thick and durable. If you choose this fabric, it may be a bit hard for you to stretch it as it remains intact. However, the great thing is that it is easier to wash and the edges are long-lived which means it does not become worn easily.

You can easily cut this fabric. You can also build blocks with quilting cotton as it allows straight matching shapes. You must pin or clip it before you start sewing. If you want to make a quilt that remains for ages, this is your pick!

2. Voile

It is a fine lightweight fabric that is soft and smooth. It has been famous in the textile industry for its flawless finish. You can use it separately as well as with quilting cotton to make a warm quilt. It is cooler and lighter than quilter's cotton; more suitable for summer. Their composition mostly contains poly-cotton blend or 100% polyester.

3. Quilter's Linen

Do you like textured types of fabric? Then, you might choose a quilter's linen. Though it is made up of 100% cotton its finish is linen-like. It does not shrink easily and is beginner-friendly to work with. It adds great interest and touch to your project.

4. Wool

Wool is a warm, toasty, and insulating material. It exhibits eccentric quality and is safe from mildew and mold. The flame-resistant fabric is not only long-lasting but also easy to cut in different patterns. However, 100% wool can be costly. Additionally, you're less likely to find patterned wool.

5. Cotton Flannel

Do you have little ones in your home? Then, flannel can be the best option. It is best suited to make quilts for newborns because of their cuddly and smooth texture. It is available in many varieties such as prints and solids. You can also combine and mix it with other fabrics too.

6. Batik

Batik is made from cotton and has versatile styles and patterns. It has many colourful and unique designs to offer. If you want to make quilts of distinctive and appealing style, batik is a great option!

Tools: Rotary Cutter, Cutting Mat, Ruler, Needles, and Thread

You need to grab a few beginner-friendly quilting tools before you begin!

- **Rotary Cutter**

The cutter works just like a pizza cuter. It has sharp blades to cut different types of fabric (thickness-wise). It is recommended to get a medium-sized cutter if you're just starting!

- **Cutting Mat**

They ease your process of cutting the fabric. A mat with a printed ruler grid is a good option. It can help you measure the fabric without any hassle. The mat with 18" x 24" dimensions would be best for freshies!

- **Ruler**

They are necessary to cut fabric accurately in length and width. For larger projects, 6" x 24" and for smaller quilts 6" x 12" rulers are a great choice.

- **Needle**

There is no such need to get sewing machine needles especially for quilting, the universal one works best. However, you should change them often for effective quilting.

- **Thread**

Using 100% cotton thread is recommended. Also, choosing a thread with colour pattern and durability in mind is essential.

- **Seam Ripper**

They are used to loosen up or open the stitches. It is herringbone Quilt Pattern Using Half-Square Triangles inevitably to make wrong stitches sometimes. So, instead of getting fed up, reverse the process with the help of seam rippers.

- **Pins**

Pins aid you in folding, holding, and adjusting fabric to keep it in place as you stitch.

These were all the essentials that are a must before you dive into the quilting realm. Now, move on to the next chapter to learn about materials!

PREPARING FABRIC FOR QUILTING

Quilts are something that lasts decades if made properly. Therefore, this guide will help you learn how to prepare, pre-wash, pre-shrink, iron, and cut fabric accurately for longevity. It is recommended to prepare your fabric for quilting when you're just about to start a project!

Washing and Ironing Fabric

Pre-washing the fabric was a thing decades ago. It is optional now as the market has introduced modern stabilisers, dyes, and good-quality fabric. Hence, there are minimal chances for the cloth to release colour or shrink. Nevertheless, there is a snippet to still help you with that!

Fabric that Need Not to be Prewashed

1. Embellished and fabric with finishing - Such cloths must remain intact to preserve the details such as embroidery or metallic accents
2. Pre-cut fabric - They make the quilting process fast and easier. They may not be washed as they are already tiny.
3. Lastly, you can also skip pre-washing if you like your quilt to be crinkled and vintage-looking.

Washing your fabric can save your fabric from dirt, preservatives, excessive dye, and chemicals.

How to Wash Your Quilting Fabric?

Separate Fabric Color Wise

Do not wash bright and dark colours simultaneously. You can wash pastels with them only if they match the family colour. The colour dye can bleed and stain other fabrics!

Cold water and Mild detergent

This can help you keep your fabric durable by saving its colour and threads!

Washing Routine

If you're using an automatic machine, settings should be at the gentlest wash. In case, you intend to hand wash, soak it in cold water for 30-60 minutes. After that, rinse it.

Drying

Ensure not to wring or twisting the fabric as it may change shape. You can use your hand to squeeze it with minimal pressure. Dry it in the shade until remains damp.

Ironing the Fabric

The final dampness should go away as you iron the fabric with a warm-hot iron setting (depending on the cloth).

Tips for Ironing

Ironing is not optional like pre-washing Therefore, you must iron your fabric before quilting for an effortless experience!

- Heat Settings - Your iron settings must be adjusted according to fabric type. Normally, the setting for cotton cloth works for various fabrics.
- Synthetic Fabrics - Such cloth type is mostly used to make quilt art or wall hanging. They can scorch or melt away due to heat.
- No steam iron - It can damage the fabric.
- Clean Iron Plate - Ensure, it's clean to not stain the fabric!

Cutting Fabric Pieces

Before you start cutting the fabric, you must choose the quilting pattern. You'll be cutting the quilting pieces according to that. It will also help you determine how much fabric you need.

Ensure, you choose an easy one as you just begin!

Get **Your Ruler**

Get a transparent acrylic quilting rule with measurements marked as 1/4" or even 1/8. They work best for straight and accurate cutting.

1. Clean Space and good lighting

Place your fabric over the mat and ensure that the light reaches the spot. You can cut the fabric efficiently by following the grid over the mat.

2. Positioning

Your fabric should be flattened out and smoothly lying over the mat. Then, follow the instructions:

- Place the ruler over the fabric.
- Ensure the scale is aligned and straightened with fabric edges and folds.

3. Cut the Fabric

Clean the excess raw edges by cutting them first. It is suggested to cut the fabric into manageable sizes if you intend to do patchwork. Cutting it in half a yard is a good idea. Once you become proficient, you can cut multiple pattern pieces at once by folding the fabric. Then, cut it at once into the desired shape.

4. Cutting

Firmly hold the cutter and make your movement slow and steady. Move down the cutter with pressure along with ruler edges over the fabric. Your fingers must not be too close as you might cut yourself.

5. Sub-cut in Desired Shapes

After cutting the fabric into manageable sizes such as long strips, you can sub-cut it in different shapes and sizes. Mostly beginners choose to cut rectangles or squares to make quilts.

Understanding Fabric Grain

Fabric grain refers to the direction in which a thread has weaved the fabric. It can be weaved length-wise, cross-wise, or bias-wise. Before that, you need to learn a few terms:

Selvedge

It is a term used to represent the tightened woven edges at the end of the fabric. It usually has holes in it too. It prevents the cloth from unravelling.

When to Use Lengthwise Grain?

When you use lengthwise grain, it usually has the least stretch. It is ideal to cut this way if you'd be hanging your quilt. It minimises sagging in your clothes and maintains stability in the quilt.

It takes more fabric and may not be ideal for quilting. The selvedge edges and length-wise fabric grain run parallel to each other. They can be a great option as:

- Efficient to cutbacks
- Left and right borders
- Applique background fabric

When to Use Cross-wise Grain?

Cross-wise grain is recommended for quilting patterns as they require selvedge-to-selvedge cutting. Crosswise grain has more stretch than Lengthwise grain. If you want to make a warm quilt which would not be hung, use crosswise grain.

It will help you economize the fabric. Also, it is stretchier than lengthwise-grain. They are ideal to make:

- Sub-cut sections
- Strips

Binding quilts (with straight edges outwards)

When to Use Bias-wise Grain

This fabric grain runs at 45 degrees from the selvedge edges. Bias-wise grains stretch more than both length-wise and cross-wise grains. You can cut the fabric bias-wise if you want to follow fabric patterns for certain strips and plaids.

You must have got a hunch about preparing the quilting fabric and cutting patterns. Let's move on to the next chapter to design your quilts!

DESIGNING YOUR QUILT TOP

Once you choose the material and learn how to prepare the fabric; the task remains to select the fabrics. The market is brimming with a plethora of designs, patterns, and colour families. For that, it can be difficult to keep your quilt attractive and appealing with so many options.

Therefore, in this chapter, you'll learn about choosing the right fabric with accurate colour and scale selection.

Choosing Fabrics and Colors

This can be your favourite part as a beginner quilter. If you want to have an easy way, I would suggest you get an already curated designer collection of fabric. This will save you a lot of time and effort. Their pre-designed collection contains well-balanced hues, scales, and contrasting prints.

Generally, the quilting cloths are chosen depending on three factors. They can vary based on contrasting colours, different shapes (dots, strips, or flowers), and the scale of the design. The balanced fabric collection must sit well together.

Choosing Color

I'd suggest you take inspiration for quilts online such as Pinterest or Quora. If you find doing this hard too, choose a single fabric with print first. Make the colours in the fabric your focus and choose other fabrics accordingly.

Looking for exact shades can be hard. Therefore, you can look for similar-looking prints with the same colour family. Ensure that chosen colours must have the same vibrancy such as bright shades or dusty, muted tones. Also, use warm or cool colors to make well pair together.

Picking Different Shades of the Same Colour

Another suggestion would be once you pick one colour, collect other fabrics from the same colour family. This way, you can add all shades of colour from brighter to lighter. This is a great way to introduce a visual interest to your quilt.

Try to refrain from making your quilt too matchy-matchy, this will make your quilt boring and flat. Zinger fabrics can also be a great option to beautify your quilt.

Choosing Fabric Scale

The size of prints over the fabric also plays a key role in your quilt visuals. Having all the fabric with large prints can make your quilt very busy look. The viewers need to rest their eyes on your art.

Therefore, always mix and match a wide range of prints from tiny ones to medium and large ones. Must add such printed fabrics which seem solid from afar, they add a great resting point to your quilt!

You can also use solid fabric when you're quilting with busy fabrics with enlarged prints. This can help them pop out nicely while neutralising the jumping hues!

Adding Texture

Another way to add a funky touch to your quilt is by using different fabrics such as linen and woven. They have different prints, scales, and design patterns. You can make a textured quilt with very similar colours but different textured patterns. It's up to you to make your quilt from minimalistic or saturated, high-colour contrast.

Always go for fabric and colour that speak to you!

Basic Quilt Blocks for Beginners

If you want your first project to be successful, ensure you cut accurately and seam appropriately. You must try again and again to follow the tutorial right away until your muscle memory learns it. If the instructions say to cut the patch to about 4" square, it must not be EXACTLY 4". Here is a list for beginners with basic quilt blocks!

1. Four Patch Unit

It is a form of patchwork done on a 2x2 grid. The four units can be unequal in size too.

2. Pinwheel Quilt Block

'This patchwork also requires you to build four patches with half-square triangle shapes.

3. Nine Patch

This is also an easy patchwork as requires you to build a 3x3 grid patchwork.

4. Autumn Tints Quilt Block

In this quilt block design, many small and large squares are arranged. You can align them according to your design.

5. Attic Window Quilt Block

This quilt work is created by a 3-D illusion. This can be done by choosing the right colours. However, one can also get a print which reflects window patterns as a beginner.

6. The Hourglass Block

This is another pattern which requires building eight half-square triangles. They can be stitched by joining triangle tips making an hourglass over a 2x2 grid.

These are a few easy-to-learn quilting ideas. Move on to the next section to create a design with me!

Creating a Pleasing Design

There are a few tips you need you be mindful of while designing your first quilt:

1. Take inspiration from your surroundings.
2. Be self-aware of your skills - see which design you can make easily.
3. Choose the quilt size - decide whether you want to design a quilt for your king-sized bed or make pillows, borders, art, or wall hangings.
4. Calculate the size of your quilt by yards - how much of the quilt top will contain patchwork, borders, or sashing.
5. Combining and contrasting colours by looking at the guide upward for patchwork.
6. Choose the fabrics - decide how you'd like your quilt to look and what would be its purpose.

1. Make Borders

Now, the actual work comes to create an actual design. Measure the fabric - by vertical midpoint, from top to bottom. Mostly quilters sew the borders straightly also known as butted borders. They are the easiest to make. Determine which width and length you'd like your border to be.

Cut it according. However, try to cut it with extra height and width of about ½ to ¼ inches, leaving space for the seams. You can use it to either cut them in length-wise or cross-wise grain. At the end, see whether the border matches the height of the quilt and cut extra edges.

Place the border strips over the quilting fabric. Pin it while measuring it from the vertical and horizontal midpoint (to make sure the equality). After adjusting, Sew borders over the fabric while leaving ¼ inch seam allowance. It prevalent bending of fabric.

Remove pins and press the stitches towards the border (More about this in Chapter 8).

2. Make Sashing and Cornerstones

The shadings are striped and make a grid layout over the quilting fabric to add patchwork. You can also add other details as needed. After that, you also need to design cornerstones that are the corners of each artwork.

3. Understanding and Designing Patchwork

The almost last task is to choose which grid patchwork you'll be working on. It refers to the arrangement of quilt blocks. There are many options like four-patch, five-patch, or nine-patchwork.

You can add all these decorative motifs and embellishments once you're done layering the quilt.

LAYERING THE QUILT:
TOP, BATTING, AND BACKING

In this chapter, we'll be discussing the making of the quilt. This segment is the backbone of the quilt. A quilt consists of three layers that are stitched together. The first layer is the top quilt (a whole cloth embellished with patchwork). The second layer is wadding/batting which provides warmth.

Wadding may consist of bamboo, natural, bleached, wool, cotton, polyester and blends. The final layer is the backing which is the button of the quilt. Here is why the layer is crucial for making a warm quilt.

Importance of Proper Layering

All quilt layers must sit properly. If they shift a bit, this can result in a wrinkled quilt from the top or the bottom. Also, the bad news is that you just can't resolve such pucker unless you do tedious unpicking. Therefore, to save you from that hassle, this section will help you with proper layering.

Here is how you can that your layers stay intact by one of these temporary methods. They only work when you're not working on a large-frame quilt.

- Tacking
- Iron-on batting
- Safety pinning
- Spray basting (more in next chapter)
- Long-arm quilter

Another key tip would be to leave extra material while you layer your backing and wadding. Make sure to leave 2 inches extra compared to the quilt top. Do this for all four sides. The thing is that the layers are most likely to creep. Hence, doing this can save you a lot of time.

Move downward to learn how can you secure smooth and wrinkle-free layers.

Ensuring Smooth and Wrinkle-Free Layers

For this, you first need to prepare your layers. Here's how you can do it!

Preparation

You need to pin the layers using normal pins to temporarily clear out the pleats and wrinkles. Iron the backing fabric and wadding to flatten them out. For large quilts, try to adjust the iron stand with a table to lay it over as a support.

Another suggestion is to lay the quilt over a flat surface overnight if you notice any fold marks in the wadding. Doing this can help them get flattened and drop out. After that, one by one flat and smooth all layers over the carpet or anywhere you feel comfortable. You can also do this activity in groups if you have quilting fellows. Do not stretch the layers!

Here are the descriptions of all available methods that ensure smooth and pucker-free layers.

1. Tacking

Tacking is a technique to hold layers together by using fluffy and weak thread. It is a time-consuming and boring task as it requires to use of tacking threads to pass it through the whole quilting cloth. Another advice would be to do long stitches from one side to another.

2. Spray Basting

This is one of the best techniques which works great for holding layers together. They are temporary adhesive sprays. They are usually used above wadding or between layers to hold their shape (more about this in upcoming chapters).

4. Iron-on Wadding

This is also an easier way to hold quilting layers. You just need to spread the quilt top, wadding and backing. Press over them according to the manufacturer's instructions. This way, the fusing medium will also get activated.

Ensure that your carpet does not release colour when heated with iron. Also, make sure to not damage the patchwork by using a thin fabric while pressing. Therefore, place another old blanket beneath all layers before ironing.

Other than that, you can also use a long-arm quilter machine, plastic tacks, or safety pins to hold the layers. Move on to the next section to learn some amazing basting techniques!

BASTING TECHNIQUES

Once you make the quilt top, the next step is to assemble them layer-wise. We learned about these in the previous chapters. In this chapter, you'll learn how you need to tack all layers. Basting is used to loosely stitch the quilt top with wadding and backing temporarily. It can be difficult for you as a beginner to smooth out all layers without wrinkles.

Therefore, in this lesson, you'll learn different basting techniques to secure the layers and prepare them for final quilting.

Using Pins or Spray Baste

Basting refers to sandwiching the batting between the designed quilt top and backing. There are three primary types the basting. Here is a detailed insight.

1. Pin Basting

It is one of the most common basting techniques to tack all layers from the quilt top of the back using safety pins. This is feasible for both large and small quilts. All you need to do is tack all layers for the whole quilt with safety pins. You may need 100+ safety pins to take the whole quilt.

Ensure to use ½ " curved basting pins. So that, they will easily pierce through all layers without leaving big holes. The gap should be minimal enough between safety pins. Such as, when you place your hand, there are safety pins within that area.

2. Spray Basting

It is an adhesive spray that works temporarily to keep all the layers aligned. Shake the bottle well before spraying it over the wrong side of both quilt top and backing. After that, make a sandwich of all the layers. Keep the bottle at a distance and spray it in a zigzag direction. This technique works faster than pin basting as you can see. It requires less than 10 minutes to spray a twin-sized quilt.

This method is not only more effective but it does not leave wrinkles behind like safety pins do. However, it is time-saving but can be costly. If you have breathing issues, you may get irritated by its smell.

Lastly, make sure to get basting spray with a "temporary tag". So that, it washes away later!

3. Fusing Spray

You can also use fusible products that melt away at very low temperatures to keep the layers together. You can place large cuts of double-sided fusible web. You can place it below and above the wadding. You can iron over to fuse the quilting layers more easily.

These were some basting techniques that ensure stability in quilting!

Ensuring Stability Before Quilting

Stabilizing the quilt is about permanently stitching the quilt which may be invisible or semi-invisible. Stabilizing ensures that the layers don't distort and stay in place. When you make stitches outlining the blocks and patchwork, it provides an infrastructure. You can start quilting your quilt anywhere from the edges or center.

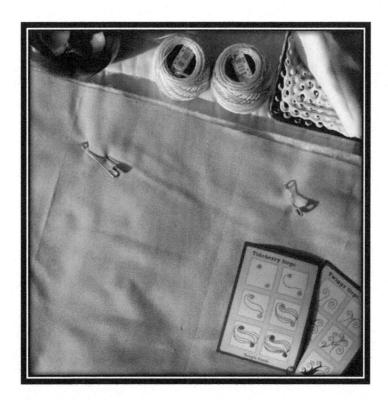

How to Stabilize a Quilt After Basting?

It is always recommended to stitch the long axis while stabilizing the quilt. You may begin by stitching the vertical axis and then go towards the horizontal ends. Also, it is useful to always stitch from top to bottom and end a very long stitching by knotting off before you go to the next row. Then, start again from top to bottom for the whole quilt.

If the quilt is too large, try to quilt the right-sided rows and shift the quilt gently to about 180 degrees. Then, you can begin stitching rows from the left side. Once you're done stitching it vertically, rotate the quilt at an angle of 90 degrees. Again, start stitching in the opposite direction horizontally.

You can either stitch by hand or with the help of a machine (more about this later in chapter 7). Before that, you must learn how to add decorative motifs on the top of stabilizing patterns. They can be added without disturbing the stabilizing stitches. Move on to the next section to learn about quilting patterns!

INTRODUCTION TO QUILTING PATTERNS

I t's time for all the patchwork you learned in Chapter 3 to get to work. Till now you must be well-accompanied in how patchwork is designed, and how borders and sashings are aligned. Now, once you're done layering and stabilising the quilt, you embellish the quilt top.

The patchwork or designed motifs are added to the top and they do not interfere with the stabilizing stitches. In this chapter, you'll learn how you can add the precut or self-designed patchwork in a beginner-friendly way!

Simple Quilting Patterns for Beginners

The quilting projects should be easy and simple in the beginning. Once, you achieve little milestones like patchwork and layering, you can amp up your game. Gradually, you can try more expert designs. However, before that learn and take inspiration from the following simple patterns for beginners!

1. Jelly Roll Jam Quilt Pattern

This is one of the easiest ways to quilt patterns without doing much. You just need to stitch three layers or strips from this pack. Make sure to cut and sew the strips in the form of a block.

2. Easy Zig Zag Quilt Pattern

This is another easy pattern to follow. In this design, you need to use 5-inch squares. If you find patchwork hard in the beginning, you can use a charm pack. To make this pattern, you just need to attach all the blocks in the zig-zag shape from top to bottom.

3. Half-Square Triangles Quilt Triangle

This is also an easier quilt pattern. This quilt design only requires you to make 10-inch half triangles. You can cut these of the same size in one go by folding the fabric. Hence, each block would be 10 inches and you'd be attaching them in opposite directions for the whole quilt.

4. Square Blocks Quilt Pattern

This pattern also requires you to join two precut strips of 10 inches to make a block. You can align them horizontally and vertically according to your choice. Just ensure, they're well-aligned.

5. Rainbow Blocks Quilt Pattern

This is another quilt design which requires you to make a block of four strips. You can make a block of 4 inches or 10 inches with prints multi-coloured in the same colour family (for each).

6. Classic Quilt Tutorial

This is another beginner-friendly quilt design. It requires you to cut 5-inch half triangles to make an hourglass. Use different printed fabrics to make an hourglass. You can sew them over the fabrics both horizontally and vertically turn by turn.

7. Plus Quilt Pattern

In this quilting design, you can use only five 5-inch blocks over a 15-inch fabric. The printed blocks should be arranged in a plus shape. This sequence can be repeated for the whole quilt making a well-designed quilt.

Now, move on to the next chapter to plan your quilting design!

Planning Your Quilting Design

There is no right and wrong way to design your quilt. It is each to their own; everyone can do what they find easy. Some people find it easier to plan quilt patterns over a page while others prefer graph paper.

Graph paper with grid lines is a great way to design your quilt pattern. The grid also makes it easier for you to shape blocks and patchwork of a certain height and width. Here are a few tips to help you design your first quilting project!

- Choose a scale - decide how many inches each block will be
- Try to start by making squares
- Draw the same quilt design multiple times before you design the whole pattern
- Calculate the block sizes and how much area they're taking. Don't forget to also draw seam allowance. This will help you learn the exact number of blocks you need to cut.
- Decide the arrangement of the blocks. Learn how the different decided shapes and patterns will go together. Remember the order of sewing while drawing the quilt
- Just to be on the safe side, only cut one block at a time for the first time. This will save you tons of fabric.
- One more useful tip is to write your pattern in your language. You can follow up with this part by adding pictures and diagrams.

Now, once you design the quilt top embellishments, it's time to get practical. Scroll down to the next chapter to learn about the stitching of the quilt!

QUILTING YOUR PROJECT

Quilting is a decade-old art. It has been around for centuries. In the earlier days, the quilts were made with the help of thread and needle by hand. However, in this modern age, you can also take the assistance of sewing machines. This way, you can get your project finished much faster.

Mostly, the patchwork is done first before layering the quilt. This is the most difficult task. After that, the layering and basting take place. Now, the time comes to sew the layers together as known as stabilize them. Some people prefer sewing by hand while others prefer using a machine. Stay tuned to learn which method suits you the best!

Choosing the Right Stitch

There are different types of stitches from which you can choose your way to quilt!

Machine Quilting

Machine quilting can be done both domestically and commercially. You can either use a simple sewing machine. Otherwise, you can get it done professionally via a long-arm quilter machine. However, it is much more costly and quilters may also not have enough space to accommodate the tool.

Long Arm or Mid Arm Quilting Machine

These machines require you to stand for a long period which can be exhausting. There are many machines in the market with advanced features. They can make your quilting process easy with professional stitching.

Hand Quilting

This is one of the most ancient ways of sewing quilts. The wall quilt arts that are found in museums now are the result of hand quilting. The hand-stitched quilts have become rare today. It is hard to find quilts produced after such hard work. Despite how old it might be, no one refuses the elegance of handpieces.

The hand-made quilting utilizes different stitching techniques. You can use different types of ways to sew all the layers of the fabric together.

Knotting

This is a popular quilting technique which keeps all layers together. This type of hand quilting requires you to use yarn thread. Then, it is passed from the backing to the top layer. Finally, securing it with a knot at the outside.

These knots provide a beautifully textured look to your quilt and also keep all layers secured. Here is a detailed comparison of both to help you choose the right stitch for your quilting project.

Hand Quilting vs. Machine Quilting

Choosing the right method for you majorly depends on your skills, project, and experience. Hand quilting consumes a lot more time than machine quilting. Here is an in-depth discussion!

Methods	Pros	Cons
Machine Quilting	Consistent and even design patterns and stitches	You may need to learn before using it properly
	Takes much less time than hand-stitching	Expensive
	Easy customization	Requires more area
Hand Quilting	Therapeutic and Relaxing	Uneven stitches
	Economic and budget-friendly	Inconsistent pattern
	Quilt everywhere you like, portable	Very time-consuming
	More artistic and inventive	Less uniform design

You can show your creativity either way. Both are great. You can also try both methods to prepare your project if you're familiar with the practices. Combining both ways can give your final product an innovative look.

Tip

A great tip would be using a sewing machine to make long stitches such as keeping all layers together. After that, employ hand quilting methods to prepare the top.

Tips for a Smooth Quilting Process

Here are a few tips you need to know for a smooth quilting process.

- Start easy and simple - It is really crucial for you to not jump into hard and large projects. Try a simple and small project such as a baby quilt. A plus point if you've got a baby at home. It takes approx. 12-15 hours to complete a baby quilt.
- Iron before basting - This is another useful tip as the top and other layers are likely to get crumbled. Therefore, make sure to give all layers a good press. So that, there are no folds later in the quilt.
- Baste well - This plays a vital role in quilting. Ensure to baste the quilt sandwich well.
- Outlining the stitches - You can mark your quilting stitches before you start sewing. You can also use a Hera marker for that. This ensures straight stitching.
- Change needles - This can smoothen your quilting process.
- Run a test - You may try to make a small quilt sandwich before you sew your patchwork over the quilt top. This will help you discern how much tension, stitch length, and pressure it requires.
- Stabilize by the center - As a beginner, you may final stitch the quilt from the center after basting. You can still do long vertical stitches but from the center this time, top to bottom.
- Take breaks - don't stress out
- Enjoy the process

The quilting process gets much more entertaining once you get familiar with the practice. After you're done making the stabilizing stitches, the next step is to add borders. Scroll down to the next chapter to learn more!

ADDING BORDERS

Quilting borders gives a great shape and structure to your quilt. They are essential for your quilt to gain stability and lay flat when done. They save you from tucks and puckers. Adding borders outlines your quilt as it divides all the sections such as designs, patchwork, appliques, and other details. Move downwards to learn about the importance of borders and more!

Importance of Borders

Borders are the strips that outline the quilt from all four sides. They form a frame around the quilt from the center. The border can be made from several patchwork squares from strips of the same fabric.

Borders provide separate sectioning to include designs, patchwork, applique, pieces, and scallops. They also increase the quilt size. They separate all design elements resulting in a distinctive design. There are also many border fabrics available that have unique fabric types and prints. They're usually designed along with the lengthwise grain.

The prints are specifically made to suit the edges coordinating for all sides horizontally and vertically. This additional factor adds beauty and balance to your quilt pattern. Borders divert viewers' attention to the patchwork that you've made with much effort.

How to Add Borders?

You must measure your quilt top before you cut the border strips. It is always better to cut the side borders first. After that, you can cut the top and bottom borders and sew accordingly. Here are the directions to cut the borders:

For Right and Left Borders

1. Measure the quilt top from the center, along the right, and left sides. Ensure to make these measurements. Never measure the borders by keeping the inches of tape at the edges as they might be folded or turned. Therefore, always measure a few inches far from the edges. The quilt must be flattened and smooth not stretched.
2. Note the measurements taken from sides vertically, horizontally, and from the center. Now, find out the average of all the calculations, this would be the ideal size of your quilt. You can decide the border width to size up or down your quilt.
3. Grab your ruler and rotary cutter to cut the strips of the border.

4. After that, fold the cut stripe of the border and quilt the top. Then, pin them both from the mid. Now, match the pinned stripe with the pinned quilt top on the right or left side. Then, pin them together from the center of the stripe from either side of the quilt top. Pin the ends too. Add a lot of pins after every 6-8 inches. This helps the borders stay intact without crumbling and in place just like all layers.

5. It's time to sew. Make medium stitches and ensure to leave ¼ seam allowance. Press the stitches to flatten them out by opening the border. Similarly, sew the border stripe in the opposite direction.

For Top and Bottom Borders

1. Measure the quilt top from top, bottom, and mid. Calculate the average of all these measurements. The result will be the length of the top and bottom borders.

2. After this, you can repeat the process as given above. Fold the stripe and quilt top horizontally. Pin and stitch according to ¼ inch seam allowance.

Tips for Adding Borders

Here are a few tips that can help you add a border to your quilt top more efficiently.

- Make measurements carefully and twice if needed.
- Make the cuts attentively.
- Use pins.
- Be mindful with sewing - you can easily get distracted while sewing large pieces.
- Start stitching from the bottom. So that, your seams and stitches look accurate and not flipped out.
- Press the border gently. So, it does not create puckers in the fabric.
- In case you're using patchwork blocks as a border, be sure to use ⅛" seam stitch for all block edges.
- There is no hard and fast rule for borders. However, it is recommended for large-sized quilts to have borders about 12-14". While small wall art borders should be approx. 6".

These were some useful suggestions to help you achieve a commendable end product. By this chapter, you must have learnt how to add borders. Now the next step is about adding the finishing touches. Now, you must ensure neatness in your project. Scroll down to learn more!

FINISHING TOUCHES

Giving the final touches to your quilt is the most important part. If you succeed in giving the final touches neatly and accurately, your final product gains value. The quality of the quilt automatically increases. They also ensure the durability of your quilt. For a quilt, the final touches after adding borders include binding, cutting excess threads, and checking seams. Go ahead to learn how can you finish the right way for your quilt!

Binding the Quilt

Binding the quilt works as a label which gives your product a professional and neat look. Here's how you can bind the quilt!

- If you want to bind your quilt, cut the strips for binding before cutting borders. This implies when you're using the same fabric for bordering and binding. You can also use most of the fabric this way. As you get to adjust the width.
- Another suggestion is to cut your binding strip using bias-grain. This will give stretch to your curved edges. It will ease the cloth at the edges.
- It is recommended to use strips or checked fabrics for binding the quilt. Also, ensure to cut them at bias. Additionally, they also add a great alluring effect to your quilt.
- When you stitch the bind to the edges, ensure to join them at the mitre joint. This will help them look put together and sit flat.
- Joint makes your quilt look hit or miss. Hence, instead of securing them with a pin to hold the shape, use metal hair slides. They will help you keep the turned joint clamped.
- For lengthwise binding other than joint corners, use pins. Tack pins every 3 inches to keep the binding attached to borders. Stitch along these pins and keep removing them as you reach them.

Here is a mini clip about how you can join mitre edges.

Trimming Excess Threads

The untrimmed and excess threads lingering around the quilt make your quilt look unfinished. They present your quilt as if there is still improvement needed. You must not waste all your efforts in the previous steps. Therefore, ensure to trim the excess threads religiously.

Gather all necessary tools such as seam ripper, needle, and scissors. Before that learn a few basic terms before getting into details:

Bobbin Thread

This thread is the bottom stitch made by a sewing machine.

Top Thread

The top thread represents the upper stitch made by the sewing machine.

Here are different scenarios to help you get away with different excess threads!

How to Get Rid of Threads from a Get-go?

The most noticeable excess threads are long tails of bobbin or top threads. If you begin here, it gets easier to bury the bobbin thread by pulling it to the top by needle. You need to pull the bobbin thread back from the hole that initiated that stitch.

There are two options. You can either bury the thread by making a knot at the bobbin thread end after making 3" stitches. Else, you may need to make a few stitches of zero length but they may result in small nests.

After that, manually trim the threads after raising them with a needle. If there are any loops, you can also use a seam ripper or scissor. Bring the bobbin loop by the seam ripper's tip to the top by the top thread. Cut them both of equal length and make a knot twice around the needle's eye. Start sewing until you reach the backing. Repeat the process until it is about to end. When it is in the middle of layers and just reaching the top, snip it swiftly and gently by breaking the thread in between.

What If Bobbin Thread Runs Out?

Here's what to do when this nightmare comes true:

- Try to unsew a few stitches back until you get enough thread. It must be enough to insert into the needle and bring it to the top.
- Pop that bobbin thread out by a needle to the top. Knot it twice.
- Cut both threads to the same length. Start sewing them through the same hole until reach the wadding and pull them out gently. This is called the quilter's knot.
- Checking for Loose Seams
- There are mostly chances for seams to become undone, You can see them at the top. So the best advice would be to stitch them together again. Try not to make the stitches from the backing to the quilt top. Try to just work over the patchwork and sew them closely. At the end, make the quilter's knot as described above leaving the thread through wadding.

If you feel that the seam is too loose, you can make a long stitch. This will help you strengthen the stitch. This way, you can save your patchwork and applique pieces too.

Here's how you can prevent these problems beforehand and not in the final touches.

Inappropriate Quilting

Batting distance refers to the stitches in quilting. Make sure to follow the manufacturer's instructions for batting distance. Usually, most suggest it to be 8-10". However, you may add more stitches if your quilt is washed and used heavily. Basting distance ensures how long the stitches can hold the layers.

The stitches get wet and dry which makes it harder for them to hold the fabric. Therefore, try to keep them close. So that, they don't get distorted easily.

Piecing stitch length

You may piece the stitch length with 1.5-2mm on the machine. This also becomes helpful to unpick later in case of poor match points. It is optional to backstitch in quilting. However, it is recommended to backstitch seams over the outer edge.

The quilt undergoes pressure while spray basting and quilting. Therefore, seams must be well-placed, tight, and extend to both ends.

Balance the Tension

You may also observe the threads from the patchwork popping out. What you may do to get rid of these? See, if there is good stitching length or quilting done. Check if the tension is balanced or not.

The threads pop out when the thread tension is at its peak. This makes the threads overstressed.

Final Pressing

Are you familiar with the "famous quilting rules"? They are all about "pressing the seams open" or "iron towards the darker side". However, it is all about preference. Some people prefer to press the seam sides. While others prefer press opening the seams. Here are a few tips for your final pressing.

Press, Don't Iron

Pressing refers to setting the iron at low pressure. It requires to put the iron over the fabric and lift from the surface. It does not involve back-and-forth motion like ironing. Pressing prevents the fabric from crumbling and puckering.

Press Stitches

Press the stitches towards the right sides once you're done with the seams. This helps your stitches sit well together.

Press Seams

If your quilt has darker fabrics, begin from there. Open their seams and start pressing in the opposite direction. Gently press them in the seam line.

Try Dry Iron

It is smoother and easier for beginners to use dry iron and splashes of water while ironing.

Finger Press the Small Details

For small patchwork and seams that can be pressed with hand pressure, sort them first.

Prevent Shadowing

The darker fabric may undershadow the lighter fabric. Therefore, press it over the darker side. For lighter fabric, open the seams. Press the lighter seams towards the lighter fabric. This ensures that both fabrics hold their look. Press seams again if needed.

These were all the details to help you with making a quilt till now. You may encounter a few problems in the future too. Therefore, there is an upcoming chapter dedicated to troubleshooting a few common issues.

TROUBLESHOOTING COMMON ISSUES

Quilting is an artistic task that is driven by creativity, desire, and passion. This perfect blend results in an extraordinary quilt. As you dive into your artistic aura, you strive for accuracy.

You try your best to pick the right fabric and build consistent design patterns, and well-aligned blocks. However, mastering quilting is a whole journey. It is not a smooth ride. Making mistakes is inevitable no matter what you do.

What matters most is that you learn from your shortcomings. Improve your skills. In this chapter, I've listed the most common issues that beginner quilters face. You'll also learn how you can tackle such problems.

Common Issues as a Beginner

The seamless quilt tops surely look amazing. However, the challenges faced by them make them that way. Here is how you can save yourself from a few common mistakes.

Dealing with Uneven Seams

The uneven stitches are usually because of poorly working sewing machines. This can be the result of the tension. This tension comes when you lay more work under the sewing machine needle than it can bear. The work meaning quilt should be lightly bunched.

If the quilt is large, the table should be set with the sewing machine. Then, gradually sew only the part needed. When you work in small bunches, it gets easier to make straight stitches. This is also a reason why people prefer free-motion stitching where they can work in small bunches. The top-to-bottom stitches get too much stress for beginners resulting in uneven seams.

The quilt may have the bulk of seam issues. Therefore, you need to ensure that the fabric is thin and pressed correctly. Also, give a good press to the seams open. These factors can eliminate the problem of uneven stitches.

Most of the time times, sewing machines have become obsolete. They either have poor stitching length (feed) or design. The machine can't hold the fabric for quilting which causes uneven stitches.

On the other hand, a few machines have too small motors. They become unable to handle the fabric weight and thickness to prepare a quilt.

One more tip would be adjusting the pressure of your pressure feet. Don't feed the machine fabric that it cannot process. Start by keeping the stitching length small such as 3" per stitch.

Do not use heavy-duty thread or needles as they can't penetrate through all layers of the quilt. It is suggested to use 60-70 microtex needles for quilting.

A few other recommendations would be proper basting. This ensures that layers do not shift causing uneven stitching. Also, you can follow the quilting guide templates for proper spacing between stitches and more. Moreover, ensure that your speed remains consistent through stitching.

Fixing Misaligned Blocks

We always try our best to buy blocks of the same size with ¼ seam allowance. However, ID blocks still differ in size what one can do? Here's how you can quickly fix this without re-seaming or re-stitching.

Quick Fix

A quick fix fix would be placing both blocks under the sewing machine's bed. Place the small one over the sides of the larger block. The even-feed foot must not be engaged over the top.

Additionally, the button teeth of the sewing machine (feed dogs) will ease the fabric while stitching. This tip only works when the block sizes differ a bit. You can't align a 1" difference. For that, there are some other practices.

What if Blocks are Too Small or large?

- Discard them and make their replacements. Ensure to leave ¼" seam allowance.
- Restitch them and ensure that you make the correct measurements this time. Use ¼" seam allowance.
- Adding borders can size up or down your block if you've made any mistakes. However, they also can't resolve a 1-2 inch difference. Borders can uniform the block sizes. You can either add them at all four sides or only the left and right sides.

Quilt blocks play a vital look in the aesthetic and design of your quilt. If they're not aligned properly, the quilt cannot stand out as much. Therefore, it is always recommended to cut precisely. Invest your time here.

Also, pin all key points strategically. So that, the stitches and seams are made properly. Lastly, ensure to press the quilt properly to help the blocks look even and flat.

Addressing Tension Issues

It is necessary to ensure that the tension is balanced while quilting. In such balanced quilting, both top and bobbin threads meet at the middle of the layers (wadding). The tension issues arise when the bobbin thread appears at the top and the top thread appears at the bottom. These problems are resolved by making the right stitches. Here's how you can do it right:

1. The first solution is to simply rethread the machine. This means that you need to remove both the bobbin and top thread and start rethreading. Ensure that you press the footer up while threading the machine.
2. Many machine manufacturers instruct you to oil and clean the innards.
3. Change your bobbin thread frequently. Make sure to use dinner thread such as monofilament or polyester.
4. Keep on testing different types of thread such as different weights for the top. Get rid of old threads that become brittle over time.
5. Choose your spool pin wisely. The vertical spool pin is used to take the parallel wound thread. While the horizontal spool pin should be used to place cross-wise thread.
6. Does your bobbin thread have appeared over the top? Then, check if the top thread tension is too tight or bobbin thread might be too loose. It can be either case. Tighten the lower thread stitch (bobbin) first.

7. If you still feel the tension in the top thread persists, loosen its tension. Keep on moving it to a lower number until it feels tightened.
8. Now see the other way around in the inner side of the top thread. If the top thread has loosened tension, tighten it. Try moving it over to a higher number.

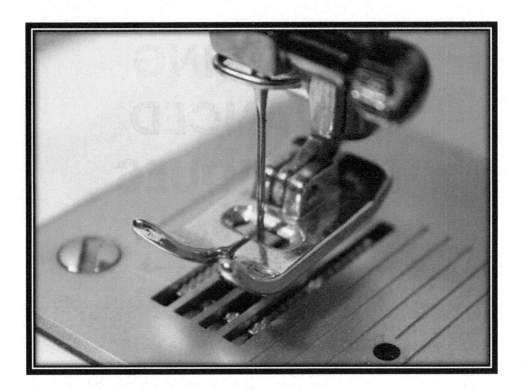

Other than that there might be these other issues:

*   Try quilting with different threads such as cotton or polyester of about 50 weights. Use the same thread for both bobbin and top stitches.
*   Check your presser foot, it might be lowered.
*   Inspect the bobbin case if there are any damages, lints, or burrs.
*   If you use a BERNINA machine, ensure not to press knee lift even a bit.
*   Clean your firmware.
*   Re-thread your top or bobbin thread.

In the beginning chapter, you learned the ropes of the quilting realm. Then, in the other coming chapters, you get familiar with patchwork and making a quilt top. After that, we got to know about layering, spray basting, and stabilizing the quilt. Moreover, you also got to know how to border and bind the quilt. Also, don't forget the finishing touches. Now that, you're also well-accompanied with the problems that might arise in the future.

It's almost time for you to enter the advanced quilting era. Move on to the next chapter to learn about more intriguing and interesting quilting techniques.

EXPLORING ADVANCED TECHNIQUES

Quilting is an art that is not limited to certain patterns and designs. You can mix and match disparate styles such as traditional, modern, contemporary, or a fusion of all. An artistic soul is always in search of making their craft top-notch. Quilters are the same. They seek different ways to explore advanced techniques that beautify traditional quilting practices.

You can try four types of quilting. The kinds include adding appliques, paper-pieced quilts, piecework, or English paper-pieced quilts to your quilt top. The piecing quilting refers to patchwork that is the most common practice for quilting. Patchwork quilting is also closely related to American quilting. In this chapter, we're about to explore top and innovative quilting techniques such as appliques, interesting embroideries, and other elements. Scroll down to discover those!

Introduction to Appliqué

Applique is a form of ornamental needlework. It involves attaching a piece of fabric that is designed to a quilt top. They can be added by hand, machine, or fused stitching. They add a personalized touch to your ending quilt. They are made of different patterns and shapes. They work as decorations over a bigger picture which is a background (such as a quilt top).

The art of applying motifs to quilts can be traced back to the 18th century. In America, the quilts were often appliqued with patchwork. The artwork consisted of alphabets, birds, or animals. In the beginning, people used to cut expensive printed fabric such as imported chintz. Then, they used to apply and pair with patchwork.

It was a celebrated quilting technique until the mid-19th century. After that, the technique was introduced to advanced styles like sentimental patterns, patriotic designs, urns of flowers, wreaths, etc. Now, applique is a worldwide technique used to adorn clothes, quilts, home decor items, design banners, and display art pieces.

This fun quilting technique is quite diverse. You can make initials and patch them over children's clothes. Also, you can apply the embellished floral motifs for quilted cushions. Before you jump into finding the applique designs, gather these basic supplies.

Basic Supplies

- **Fusible web** - This works as a gluing agent to stick the fabric and motif together. This is ideal for applique, applying borders, hemming, and craft work. The web works as a middleware to stick the applique patch with the quilt. It is an easier and cheaper way to apply while saving time.

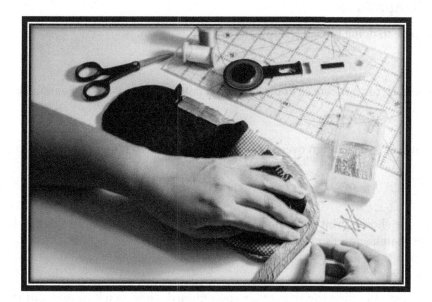

If you fail to get an affordable fusible web then you can also get spray fabric glue. It also works amazingly to stick the patches. This way is ideal for raw edge fusible applique (stay tuned).

- **Iron** - In hand applique, heat is needed to activate the fusible web mostly. Hence, low-heated iron is appropriate for this task.

Or

- **Iron-on Interfacing** - Just like fusible webbing, this is another way to stick the design to a quilt top. Both ways utilize iron heat to melt and activate the glue. However, in this way, the fabric is used as a sticking agent instead of plastic-like fusible webbing. Iron-on interfacing is preferred while doing inside-out applique (scroll to learn more).

Other than that, equip yourself with needles, thread, and fabric. There are three ways you can attach your applique patterns by hand.

1. Raw Edge Fusible Appliqué

Here is a step-by-step guide to doing raw-edge applique:

Step 1:

Cut the fusible web according to your chosen applique design pattern. Ensure it is big enough to cover the whole area.

Step 2:

Draw and outline the shape of your design over the paper side of the web. You can make a leaf, heart, flower, square, or any shape you like.

Step 3:

Place the web side over the chosen print or fabric to applique while facing the paper side up. Let them sit, adjust and fuse. You may follow the manufacturer's instructions here.

Step 4:

Now, once it cools down, start cutting the shape that you outlined. Now, you'll have to cut the fabric in the desired shape to be appliqued with the fused web.

Step 5:

Peel the paper off the shape from the bottom of your design. If you find it difficult to scrape it off easily, try using pins and then peel it off gradually.

Step 6:

This is the most important step where you need to place the cut applique pattern over the fabric. Ensure, it seems appropriate over the background fabric like a quilt top. Eventually, use iron to paste the design. The iron must be low to medium heated.

Step 7:

The last step may need to be clarified. It requires you to stitch the outer edges of the applique design. For this, you can either use hand stitching, machine stitching, or top stitching close to the edge. This step is necessary to secure the shape.

Here are a few hits and misses:

Pros

- Best to applique complicated shapes
- Flat and cleaner look
- You can employ both hand or machine stitching
- Easy and quick

Cons

- Fusible web and iron required

2. Inside Out Applique

Here's how you can try this technique in detail:

Step 1:

Cut the fabric and the interfacing according to the size of the chosen shape. However, ensure to cut it a bit bigger and leave at least ¼ inches around all the sides.

Step 2:

Place the interfacing over the fabric. Place the template or outline the shape you want them to cut into.

Step 3:

Now, place the pins across two sides of both the interfacing and fabric to hold them. Start machine or hand stitching them around the outline and all edges.

Step 4:

Cut the stitched and outlined piece leaving 1/8-1/4 inch seam. If your shape is smaller then the seam allowance would be lesser and the curves would be more acute. Do not cut through stitching.

Step 5:

Be careful in this step and cut only in the interfacing from the mid making a slit. Ensure not to disturb any stitches in the edges. Roll out the edges and smoothen out the curves by pushing them.

Step 6:

Press over the interfacing. Make sure that you can still see the fabric through the interfacing and the edges. This helps ensure that interfacing won't flow out of the applique patch.

Step 7:

Place and position the design over the background fabric. You might use the shape template to make the right adjustments and place it in the center.

Step 8:

There are two options to either top stitch close to the edge or by hand around the shape corners.

Now, if you want to apply more critical designs like **stems and vines** with the inside-out method, here's how you can do that.

Stems and Vines Applique by Inside-out Method

In this tutorial, you'll learn to add flowers and create stems and curve vines.

Note: This series only works if you're using an inside-out technique. For raw edge, you can use a similar guide to create stems, vines, and knotty designs.

Step 1:

Use bias-wise fabric grain to cut the stem from your desired fabric. Ensure to cut it twice in width you'd like the final stem to look like. Also, don't forget to leave ¼ inch for the seam.

Step 2:

Fold the strip to stitch it leaving a ¼ inch seam.

Step 3:

Now, fold the strip to make the seam part sit at the back and smooth the fabric over the front line. In case your trip is less wide than 1 inch, you may need to cut the raw edges from the seam. So, they don't show up in the front.

Step 4:

Press the rolled strip well. This will make the stitches sit in place.

Step 5:

Now, place the strip over the background fabric. Here, you can use pinning and technique techniques to change the shape of the strip temporarily. This will hold the strip as you stitch it later. Press the curves later.

Step 6:

Find a matching thread and stitch the strip along its edges over the fabric.

Here are a few pros and cons of the inside-out applique method.

Pros

- Creates a turned-edge look
- You can employ both hand or machine stitching
- Overall similar to needle turn but gives a three-dimensional visual to your quilt

Cons

- You need iron
- You require a thin interfacing material to fuse the fabrics
- This is it, move forward to learn about needle turn applique.

3. Needle Turn Appliqué

Here is a step-by-step guide.

Step 1:

Get your background fabric and outline the desired shape on its wrong side. You can either use the template or outline the shape by drawing.

Step 2:

Now, cut the fabric to be appliqued ¼ inch bigger than the shape size from all edges. You may choose flowers, leaves, and stems for this part.

Step 3:

Now, place the cut pieces over the background fabric's right side. Tack and pin the patches. So that, they can hold their position.

Step 4:

Use a thick needle and old thread to make reverse stitches from the wrong side of the background fabric. Follow the outline made on the wrong side. So that, you'll automatically leave the ¼ inch to turn all edges at the end.

Step 5:

Finally, tie a knot to secure the thread in the applique's shape and tone up the pattern.

Step 6:

Try to unpick the tacking stitches one or two and pass through the raw edges of the applique piece. Press and hold the edge in a curved position. Take the needle through the fold and across the background fabric. Then, position the needle in the direction of the applique pattern slightly.

Step 7:

Now, leave ⅛ inch seam allowance and then move the needle again in the upward direction. Similarly, switch the angle by moving back into the background fabric. Repeat this process by moving around the shape, unpicking the stitches, and using a needle to fold the raw edges. Following it by pressing the edges under your fingers and making invisible stitches.

Here's why you may or may not choose a needle-turn applique.

Pros

- Suitable for stitching on the go
- Traditional approach
- No additional tools required

Cons

- Stitching by hand only

Do you want to advance your quilt and appliques game? Then, you may also experiment with embroidery.

Experimenting with Quilt Embroidery

Adding embroidery to your applique is a great way to add a personalised touch to your quilt. This technique and step can be expert-level. Nevertheless, if you have successfully made 1-2 basic quilting projects (more in the next chapter), you can hop on this later.

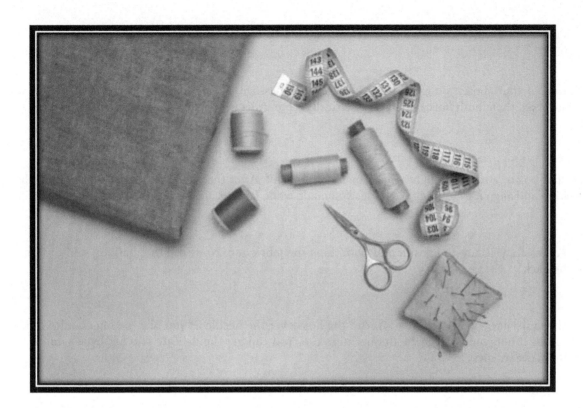

Here are which and why supplies are needed in quilting embroidery over the applique. This step comes after you have applied the motif or patch to the background fabric as given above.

1. Embroidery Hoop

Embroidery hoops tighten the fabric over which you'd be embroidering. They flatten and smoothen out the cloth. So that, you stitch evenly and consistently. They come in a variety of sizes from 3" to 12" in diameter. You can get yours according to your applique size. We'd suggest getting the medium 7" diameter hoop.

Ensure to grab the hoop which has an interlocking tongue and groove. This prevents your fabric from slipping away during the process.

2. Embroidery Hand Needles

Embroidery needles come in a variety of sizes. The larger the size, the thinner the needle and its eye. Though, the higher number of needles makes accurate stitches they might be tricky for beginners. Therefore, try to experiment with different needles over unnecessary fabric

3. Cotton Floss (six-strand)

Cotton floss is often used to paint the embroidery. It is used to make cross, satin, and long-and-short stitching projects. They are used to beautify the surface embroidery. The floss may get tangled or tossed. Therefore, you might need to be attentive when using cotton floss while embroidering.

4. Marking Tool

Marking tools are the most efficient best friends when you're just learning the ropes. Unless you wish to try free-form embroidering, be sure to outline or mark your design. This speeds up your overall embroidering and tracing process later. Also, the stains from the tools mostly fade in a few days.

Other than that, grab the fabric to work on, small scissors, and a sewing box to store all the accessories.

Step 1:

Get a printout of your chosen design which can be initial, message, or anything. Draw the shape of the applique to your printout. Fold them both horizontally and vertically. Later, this will make lines over to help you align your design efficiently.

Step 2:

Use a flat light box or a source of light. Tape down the printout. After that, align and set the fabric over the light and paper. Position and align it following the creases you made while folding.

Step 3:

Once you successfully secure the position of both, tape the fabric too. Now, use the marking tool to trace down the design in the back.

Step 4:

Let's start the embroidery now. Ensure to thread the floss over the needle. If you like the big chunky stitches, use all six floss strands. If not, you can get the thinner ones too. You can get the delicate stitches by separating the strands and using them eventually.

Step 5:

Cut your floss about the length of 12" – 18". Ensure that the length at most should be from the tips of your fingers to inside the elbow. Any floss longer than this length can result in tiredness and aching hands. This can be because you pull the floss back and forth to make even stitches. There are chances of knotting while using long-length flosses too.

Step 6:

If you want thick stitches, you need to pass the six strands from the needle eye. This can be tricky. Therefore, the suggestion would be to cut the tip to 45 degrees. Also, humble the strands by wetting them a bit. This makes them lose their sturdiness and get soft. Now you may insert the needle.

Step 7:

Make stitches according to your desire. Watch this video if you wish to embroider initials or alphabets.

There is much more to this fun technique applique. Move on to the next section to learn how to make the applique three-dimensional.

Incorporating Three-Dimensional Elements

It is a form of embroidery known as foam or puff. It is used to add batting or some fabric to the applique pieces. So that, the appliqued shapes can rise above from background fabric giving a 3-D effect. Here's what you need to do!

Gather fusible web and background fabric (can be cotton). You can choose any fabric type like batiks, solids, or prints. Endure to take the fabric in double quantity as the applique shapes are going to be double-sided. Here are a few steps you need to follow:

- Lay parchment paper over the iron board to save the fabric.
- Cut the chosen fabric according to the size of the shape or pattern. Ensure to cut it twice as the shape size as it would be double-sided. Cut the fusible web of the same shape and size (also double in size). Attach it to the wrong side of the applique fabric.
- Use a dry and hot iron to attach the fusible web to the fabric. Press and hold for 8 seconds for each cycle.
- Let it cool down and peel off the paper from the upper side of the web.
- Fold the fabric with the fused web together. Now, you will see it's double-sided.
- Outline the shape you'd like to applique. Cut the double-sided fused fabric accordingly. Press it again. So that, it holds the shape for you. Let it cool down.
- If you wish not to flatten them, you can change the dimensions and reheat the shape.
- Use your fingertips to make it look more curved and rising from the background fabric.
- Finally, if there's a flower, you can stitch it from the center over the background fabric. This will leave the edges floating giving your applique a 3-D look. We'd suggest using a big needle to stitch the 3-D elements to the quilt.

QUILTING BASIC PROJECTS

It is not an easy task to sew a whole quilt. The beginners can get overwhelmed by the rigorous patchwork, layering, tacking, stabilizing, and stitching the fabric. Therefore, it is crucial for all those just getting their feet wet to take it slow. Start with easy and small projects.

Once they achieve success in making mini quilts, they can move towards intermediate and expert-level designs. The great thing is that both the large and small quilting projects involve the same steps of making. The only difference is that small projects can be handled by newbies easily.

1. Simple Patchwork Quilt: Start with squares or rectangles to create a basic patchwork design.

Here's how you can create a simple and beginner-friendly square patchwork. You can also change cutting variations and sizes to rectangles to try different patchwork patterns.

Instructions

- Choose a printed fabric for squares. Cut it into 10 inches in square form. Cut them in half. Now, the shape would be rectangular. Try to choose different prints.
- Now, choose a plain and solid fabric and cut the squares. Keep the variations for 10 inches by 9.5 inches on each side. Also, ensure to trim them more by keeping the measurements about 9.5 by 2.5-inch strips.
- Now, stitch two printed rectangles together. Try to use a scant ¼ inch seam allowance.
- Press the edges of the rectangular blocks and try to trim them into 9.5-inch squares.
- Make the cut pieces according to the size of your project. Repeat the process of stitching two different rectangles into squares. Lay all your patterns on the floor to determine the pattern and layout of the patches.
- Now, take the white strips cut above and sew them row-wise with each square. After each square, sew the strips. Then, after stripping another square. Repeat the process for all rows. Press the seams flat towards the coloured pattern.
- Similarly, as above, the sashing would be added column-wise too. This will separate all the squares.
- Cut the strip yardage according to the length of your quilt with the same measurements as row-wise. Sew this strip between all rows. Don't forget to cover the top and bottom of the quilt too.
- Tada, baste and sandwich all layers.

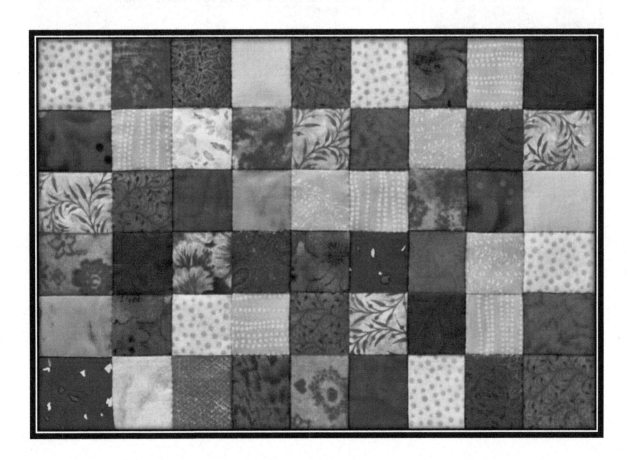

2. Rail Fence Quilt: Utilize strips of fabric to create a simple yet visually appealing design.

This design would be for a baby quilt 40x40 inches. Here's how you can make a rail fence quilt.

Instructions

- You need to grab four different prints for this project. You'll need half a yard of all these fabrics.
- Cut all these fabrics into long strips with 2 ½" width. Take five strips out of all the fabrics making 20 strips in total.
- Now, sew them together by using a scant one-quarter-inch seam allowance. Start with two and eventually sew the five strips together. Press the stitches in one direction.
- Now, place the ruler over the sorted and sewn strips. Cut them into squares with measurements 8 ½" x 8 ½" square. You'll get the final 5 square blocks at the end of one set.
- Now, repeat the process for the remaining strip sets. This will result in 25 identical blocks.
- Lay all blocks side by side. However, this twist is to change the direction. From one block keep the strips horizontal and then vertical. Repeat the sequence. Ensure, to press the seam toward the vertical block.
- Assemble the second row similarly. Make sure that you observe the rail fence pattern.
- Use 1 ¼ yards of plain fabric for backing. Baste and stabilize the quilt.
- Finally border the quilt with 4 strips 2 ½" for all the sides. Use bias-fabric grain to cut the borders. Sew them end-to-end.

3. Nine-Patch Quilt: Learn the basics of piecing together nine squares for a classic quilt block.

This quilting project can be used as a table topper. In this quilt, you can either use precuts too. Their measurements can be 5″ or 2 ½″ squares.

Instructions

- Take a charm pack and grab 21 5″ square blocks. Cut them into four pieces making the length and width of each 2½″ square. Repeat for all other squares.
- Randomly mix and match about 9 blocks with 2 ½″ inch size. You'll see 9 sets of 9 mini square blocks.
- Sew the three blocks row-wise. Use, a scant ¼″ seam allowance for making all the stitches. Press the seam out. Repeat the process and sew the other three blocks set row-wise but press the seams inside. Finally, for the last three blocks sew them row-wise and press seams outside.
- Now, sew all these three rows to make a nine-patch. Press the seams to opposite sides to make the corners of the nine-patch prominent.
- Press after stitching. Repeat this process for the remaining 8 blocks of nine patches.
- Add sashing row and column-wise with measurements 1¾″ wide. You'll need six strips to cover both row and column-wise.
- Cut the strips about the length of the nine-patch block. Stitch them between the blocks leaving ¼ inch allowance. Press the stitches towards the strips. Now, you'll have three rows consisting of 9 patches stitched via sashing.
- Now, add the sashing strips to the top, bottom, and in between the rows. Cut them according to the quilt size. Press the seams towards the sashing.
- Pin, baste, and tack. Your quilt is ready!

4. Herringbone Quilt: Experiment with arranging rectangular pieces in a herringbone pattern.

Creating this quilt can be difficult because of its tricky shape. However, this is one of the easiest projects once you accurately cut the shapes. The great thing is that the additional sashing is not needed!

Instructions

- In this project, you need 380 pieces to make a throw quilt. You can minimize the quilt size by reducing the pieces. All pieces would be 2 ½ inches wide. Their length would be 8 inches from point to point.
- Divide these pieces into two parts. Half of them should be of solid color preferably light colour. The other half can be of any printed fabric. Now, half of both parts should be cut at a mirrored angle to make the herringbone shape.
- Layer 5 fabric strips over each other on a cutting mat to cut them simultaneously.
- Place the ruler over the strips and cut at a 60-degree angle vertically. Then, move the ruler to 8 inches and cut the first strip at a 60-degree angle. Repeat this process for both plain and printed fabric until you achieve 95 strips from each.
- Now, cut the remaining 95 pieces in a mirroring direction. You will repeat the same process but just start cutting the strips from the wrong side of the fabric.
- Now, the tiring part begins, lay out all the pieces in the herringbone arrow direction. Pair the solid pieces with printed pieces. The mirrored angle once would be put against the normal pieces. If you're working with 380 pieces, you are likely to have 10 columns with 38 pieces in each.
- You can stack all columns over each other. Pin the pieces and name the column if not sewing the same day. Keep the corresponding columns together. So that, you're not mistaken.

- Place the opposing pieces over each other. They should not align and must leave ¼ inch corners outside from both sides.
- Now, start by stitching them column-wise. Start with straight stitching them along the edges while leaving ¼ inch seam allowance. Repeat the process until you complete 38 pieces. Do it until you get 10 columns.
- Now, stitch the opposing columns together with the right sides. Pin them to secure the layers temporarily. Similarly, stitch them leaving ¼ seam allowance and remove the pins eventually. Repeat until you finish all the pieces.

5. Log Cabin Quilt: Explore the traditional log cabin block for a timeless design.

This is a mini quilt project. Here are the instructions to make a log cabin quilt.

Instructions

- You'll be cutting 13 strips with different lengths and the same width of 2.5". Cut them all with lengths such as one stripe of 14.5", two of 12.5", 10.5", 8.5", 6.5", 4.5", and 2.5" respectively. Ensure to take a variety of solid-coloured fabrics.
- Log cabins mostly begin from the center. So, start by stitching the two strips of 2.5" side by side. Don't forget to leave ¼ inch seam allowance. You don't need to make the seams align so press them open.
- Now, it's time to take the two 4.5" strips and stitch them to the previously stitched logs. Place one stripe below the 2.5" pieces and stitch with ¼ allowance. After that, take the other one and stitch at the right side of the sewn logs.
- Ensure that you stitch them in a log shape. Now, for the next round take a 6.5" stripe. You can try different colors such as warm or cool tones. Stitch this stripe at the top of the log block created.
- For the next 6.5" stripe, stitch it along the left side of the log block.

- As we're doing counter-clockwise, now the step comes to stitch an 8.5" long log. Stitch it at the end of the block. For the second 8.5" long stripe, stitch at the right side of the block.
- Then, repeat the process by stitching a 10.5" long log at the top. Then, the other 10.5" stripe on the left.
- Then, keep on going by sewing the first 12.5" log at the bottom. Also, the other one should be stitched on the right side.
- Finally, the 14.5" long log should be stitched at the top completing the log cabin. Now, you can double the lengths and widths for a bigger quilt. Ensure to stitch while leaving a ¼ seam allowance. This is it!

6. Chevron Quilt: Create a modern look by arranging fabric in a chevron or zig-zag pattern.

This is one of the easiest-looking quilts. However, making the measurements and placement can be tricky. Therefore, having precuts with you can make this work easier. Here you go:

Instructions

- Take pre-cuts for a 5 ½" square. Ensure that all strips are 2 ½" wide. Do not use wider or narrower stripe sizes as they might change the chevron look.
- Take 4 strips out and cut them 2 ½" inch wide. Cut them across the fabric width. Stitch two pieces together making a set of two stitched patches. Press seams to one side for both sets of two strips.
- Start stitching along the edges by placing both sets upside down by right sides. This way, you'll form a tube. Don't worry, the fabric will open up as you cut them via corners.
- Now, place the ruler at the 45-degree angle over the right lower corner of the tube. Cut the triangle and discard it (you can also keep it in the basket and use it later).
- Now, flip the ruler and you'll notice a triangle at 45 degrees in the upper right corner. Cut it and open the fabric. You'll notice a chevron pattern. Repeat the process to get more chevrons.

- Each tube will result in two chevron blocks. You can make two more of these to complete the block. You can size up or down accordingly.

7. Pinwheel Quilt: Master the technique of creating pinwheel blocks for a playful design.

This is a tutorial to make a four-patch pinwheel design. Once you complete one piece, you can try this on a larger scale. Here's how you can make a pinwheel quilt.

Instructions

- Get four squares of 2-3" measurements. Ensure to take two squares of dark colour and the other two of light tones. Cut them all diagonally from the mid. Now, you'll have eight half-square triangles (HST).
- Align the HST blocks of different tones together. Stitch them making a square leaving one-quarter seam allowance. Repeat for all blocks. This way, you'll get four squares of both light and dark tones matched.
- Take all four HST block squares and align them to make another big square.
- Firstly, stitch a set of two blocks column-wise. Similarly, repeat for the second set two. Now, stitch both sets row-wise making a pinwheel design. You can make plenty of these to complete a bigger quilt.

8. Diamond Quilt: Experiment with diamond-shaped pieces to create an elegant quilt.

Making a diamond quilt may seem hard but it's not. You may learn how to cut the diamonds first to make a diamond quilt. Here is what you need to do!

Instructions

- Take 2 ½" wide and long-length strips of different printed or solid fabrics.
- Take a ruler and cut them at 60 angles from the lower selvedge. Discard the fabric. Now, keep the ruler position the same (tilted). Grab your rotary cutter and start cutting diamonds at 2 ½ distance. Repeat the process until you reach the end of the stripe. You can line up the strips and cut them at once. By keeping the ruler at them at once at 60 degrees.
- You can take a row of diamonds from different fabrics. Then, stitch them side by side from the bottom column-wise. This way you you'll get corner-by-corner columns of diamonds. You can start by stitching them with this setting in mind.

Number of columns	Diamonds to be stitched
2	2
2	4
2	6
2	8
2	10
2	12
2	14
2	16
2	18
2	20
2	22
2	24

5	25

After you finish making the columns and stitching them in rows. The next step is to stitch the rows together leaving ¼' seam allowance. Press seams toward the smaller row.

Once, you complete all rows, you'll get a stretchier quilt as the diamonds were cut using bias-wise grain.

Finish off by basting, quilting, and adding borders to the final quilt.

9. Brick Wall Quilt: Arrange rectangular pieces to mimic the appearance of a brick wall.

This is a quilt tutorial for a 63″ x 84″ size. Here's how you can get yourself a brick wall design.

Instructions

- It would be easier if you get two white charm precut squares with a 5″ size. Also, 42 pieces of printed squares of about 10″ size. Cut these 42 squares in half making them look like rectangles.
- Now, take those white squares from charm packs. Stitch to the cut rectangles at one end. You'll repeat the process for all 84 rectangles. Ensure to press the seam towards the colored fabric.
- Lay about 14 of these stitched rectangles row-wise side by side. Do not place them in the same direction. Change the direction of each with respect to the corresponding rectangle (upside down). Leave ¼ seam allowance and stitch them side-by-side. Press the seams to the left side for odd rows (1, 3, 5). For even rows, press the seams to the right side.
- Sew these rows horizontally.

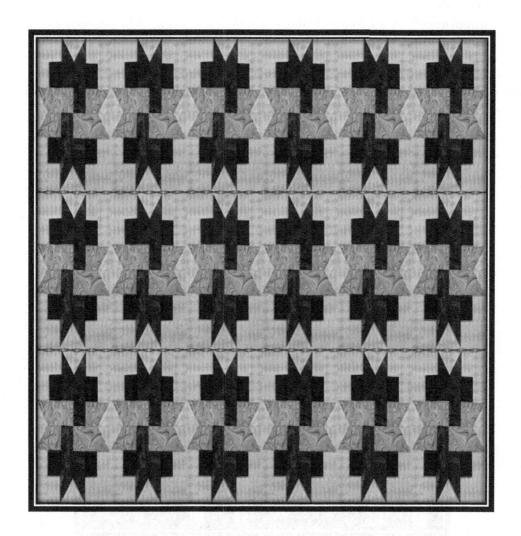

10. Strippy Quilt: Practice sewing strips of fabric together for a straightforward yet lovely quilt.

This strippy quilt does not require much work. You just need to handle a lot of fabrics to make this quilt. There are steps given below to help you make one.

Instructions

- You need to get eight types of fabric with different colors and prints. Take seven of these of about ⅓ yard. Lastly, take 1 ½ yards of white fabric which will be used as a background from all colorful strips. Your quilt will be approx. 58" x 72".
- From the colorful fabrics, take 2 pieces of 6" inches out. For the white one, there should be 9 pieces with the same measurements.
- Now, take the colourful strips and cut one up to 40 inches long with the same 6-inch width. Again, cut strips 20 inches long with 6 inches width.
- For the white fabric, cut six strips with a length of 40 inches and a similar 6-inch width. The remaining three should be 20x6 inches.
- Now, take stripes from the same coloured fabrics. Sew both the 40 and 20 inches vertically side-by-side. Try to stitch one strip in the opposite direction to another. For instance, you're sewing a red 20-inch strip with a red 40-inch on the left. Then, for the blue one stitch it along the right side, and repeat the process. Repeat for all the strips. You'll end up with six white fabric strips and six colourful ones.
- Arrange them as they were stitched with opposite sides vertically. There is your quilt pattern, stitch them horizontally across the width. Finish off with binding and quilting!

This chapter covers all beginner-friendly quilting projects. After you get a good grip here, move on to the next chapter. The upcoming section contains some intermediate projects!

QUILTING INTERMEDIATE PROJECTS

Now that you're done with shapes, it's time to game up. An avid quilter must have disparate designs in their collection. Therefore, this chapter covers something beyond just shapes and their placement. In this lesson, you'll learn a lot of new quilting patterns. So, move down to get to work!

1. Sampler Quilt: Combine various quilt blocks to create a sampler that showcases different techniques.

Sampler quilts usually consist of different numbers of blocks such as six or nine. They all have different patchwork. Here's how you can make this one easily.

Instructions

- Make squares or blocks from all the shapes and designs learned in the previous chapter. For instance, take 9 design samples from that chapter and stitch them to make a quilt.
- Ensure to make them of the same size such as 10x10". You can size up and down depending on your needs.
- In sampler quilts, the designed artwork is usually separated by sashing both horizontally and vertically. In these quilts, you also have to add borders and binding.
- Make sure to stitch three previously designed pieces side by side by sashing in between. The length of the sashing must be similar to the block size. You can keep the width 2 inches. Then, repeat the process until you get three rows. Each will consist of three different patterns.
- Now, add sashing horizontally along the width and stitch the rows. Repeat till all rows are done. Finally, move on to the sashing and border chapter for detailed tips and tricks. You're done. Make this work easy for you by making the project miniatures discussed earlier.

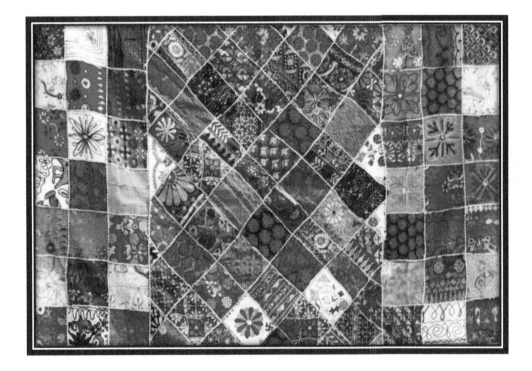

2. Bargello Quilt: Explore the art of bargello quilting with its striking wave-like patterns.

This quilt pattern can be different from the previous designs. In a bargello quilt, you'll be cutting the strips width-wise. The design requires you to make waves. They are achieved by different colour groups. In this tutorial, we'll be using two colour groups that can range from lighter to darker shades. Here are a few instructions and tips to help you get there.

Instructions

- Select any two colour groups and take ten coloured fabrics from each group. Sort them from darker to lighter shades from the right side. You need four sets of 20 strips with 2 ½ width.
- As discussed, arrange them from the right side with darker to lighter shades. Now, start stitching the first set of 20 strips length-wise. Leave ¼ seam allowance.
- Stitch the strips together. After that, press them in opposite directions according to their colours.
- Cut the strips horizontally with 2 ½ width. Cut the strips one by one from all sets of loops.
- Now, remove the stitching between fabric 1 and 2 strips. Make a loop by stitching to the second slice in the strip set. Then for the second strip, stitch the end of the strip to the third slice and unpick the seams between fabric strips 2 and 3. Continue this process for the remaining strips.
- Now lay these fabric strips. You'll notice a wave pattern. Stitch them horizontally upside down side-by-side. Stitch until you reach the final strip and your quilt design is ready. Layer and baste properly!

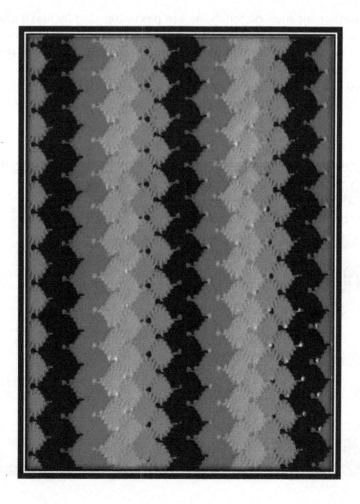

3. Double Wedding Ring Quilt: Take on the challenge of piecing together interlocking rings for a classic design.

These types of quilts often make a great wedding gift. Making them does not require a ruler. However, you need cutting templates to get the right shape. Before you begin, ensure to select your fabric, template size, and pattern.

Instruction

- Get center and melon templates. When you use the center template over the fabric, the remaining corner fabric will make four melons. You can put the melon template over the scrap fabric to accurately get the melon shape.
- Keep cutting both shapes until you reach 100 center pieces and 220 melon pieces.
- Now, the turn comes to cut the squares and wedges. Now, if you've scrapped strips, you'll find this part amazing.
- You can use 2" strips to cut our square shapes. Also, you can use 2 ½" strips to make wedges. Try to pick light-coloured fabric to make squares and wedges. Cut 440 pieces of the square shape. Now, it may sound straining but you need to cut 2640 wedges. This is a wedding ring quilt. So, hang in there!
- Now, it's time to make the rings from the 2 ½" wedges. They will have narrow and wide edges. You should stitch them together. Stitch the narrow and wide ends side by side with ¼ seam allowance. Iron after you get done with every six pieces. Stitch the first six pieces together. Then, make a batch of those. Then, join them. Stack them layer-wise and pin them. So that, they hold the shape. Stitch the melon corners within the curve made by six wedges.
- Now, repeat the procedure for squares. Stitch the 440 pieces together by making batches of 8 at a time. Now, press these squares and stitch them over the other side of the melon stitched to wedges.
- Stitch them at the corner of the center that we cut at the beginning. About 4 of the melons would be stitched to the center. Do not stitch beyond the seam.
- Now, it's time to make the pattern out of the stitched shapes. Start stitching the other center pieces to the upper edges of the melon. So, you need to make one melon and continue the design with other pieces. Check in again and again to see if any loopholes.

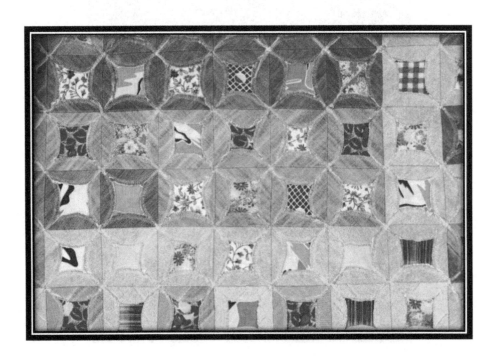

4. Dresden Plate Quilt: Practise curved piecing and appliqué to create beautiful Dresden Plate blocks.

This is also an easy quilt project. Here's what you need to do.

Instructions

- Take 16 pieces of 13" fabric and cut them using a blade template. Press them and fold them vertically. Iron the upper wider inches of the fabric to flatten the fabric. This will create a crease.
- Now, fold it from the midpoint and both sides a bit making a pointed shape. Stitch the upper folded edges.
- Repeat the process to make 15 more pieces. Finally, add the fabric in the middle. It is a kind of applique quilt pattern. So, create many such pieces and needle applique later.

5. Sunburst Quilt: Experiment with radiating patterns to create a sunburst effect in your quilt.

This quilt looks like sun rays shining over all things. For this tutorial, we'll be making a picnic rug quilt. Here's how you can make this one!

Instructions

- Take a yard of fabric from seven different colours from the same school. Now, take a sample quilt of the size you'd like your quilt to be.
- Find a point a bit far from the mid and close to the bottom. Mark that point. Now, start making rays of different lengths and widths. You can do that randomly. Try to make a place for at least 7 rays from 7 fabrics. Mark these spaces with numbers. Now, cut the fabrics according to the marked lines. This will be half of the quilt. Stitch the layers side by side, they will look like pointed long triangles. Stitch them from those points together. Leave ¼ inch seam allowance.
- Now repeat the same layers for the bottom quilt. Stitch them along the mid to the ending points.
- Baste and quilt properly.

6. Appliqué Quilt: Master the art of appliqué by adding intricate fabric shapes to your quilt top.

Making this quilt can be easier for you if you've mastered making appliques. Follow the instructions below to learn more.

Instructions

- Choose your background fabric. Choose the number of motifs you'll be adding to the fabric. Your options can vary from pebbles, flowers, feathers, meanders, swirls, or paisleys.
- Make appliques by following the guide in the "Advanced Techniques" chapter. Ensure to leave ⅛ seam allowance.
- After that, decide on sashing, cornerstones, and borders. Don't forget to baste and quilt.

7. Attic Windows Quilt: Create the illusion of windows using contrasting fabrics for a three-dimensional effect.

This is 3-D work. You need to follow these instructions to get an attic window quilt.

Instructions

- Take three fabrics of different colours. Cut ¼ yard of fabric for each.
- Cut 2" squares, a 2x6" rectangle, and a 6x6" square. Ensure to cut the squares and rectangles from different fabrics. This means one fabric would be used to cut a square and a rectangle with a given size. Then, use another fabric for the second batch.
- Cut the 2" squares in half making two triangles.
- Now, stitch the half triangles from different fabrics from the mid. Leave ¼ inch seam allowance and open them from the center. This will again result in a square.
- Now, stitch the triangle with rectangles of the corresponding colour. Stitch one rectangle on the left side-by-side. Attach the other one to the top of the square. Then, for the remaining space, stitch the 6" square. Make such patterns multiple times enough to cover the whole quilt.

8. Pineapple Quilt: Challenge yourself with foundation paper piecing to construct pineapple block patterns.

Do you have any 1 ½" strip scrap? Then, you'd be glad to learn that you make this pineapple quilt easily.

Instructions

- Cut four strips of about 1 and ½ inches wide and 6 inches tall. Ensure to cut them from 2 different fabrics; two red and 2 blue strips. Make a "V" of two strips diagonally. Then make the "^" shape of the remaining strips and place them over the "V" diagonally.
- Place the ruler with ¼ inch mark over the strips. Cut the outward edges. Cut a 2x2 square and place it between the setting of strips. Stitch the strips like that making a diamond. Press the pieces as you get done.
- Now, take other strips about the width of the strips. However, this time with a 4-inch length. Stitch them, in the gap between the strips. Then, place the square in the middle. Place the square in the opposite direction like a diamond over the square.
- You can build this pineapple more by adding longer strips around.

9. Stack and Whack Quilt: Learn the technique of stack and whack to create kaleidoscope-like quilt blocks.

This quilting project can be a bit tricky. Here are a few tips to help you get the stack and whack quilt.

Instruction

- Take eight square stacked layers identical from the same fabric. Cut those into halves diagonally. Now, there would be 16 identical triangles. Now, the easier way would be appliqueing these shapes over a background fabric.
- Start from the mid and start stitching horizontally and then all the remaining triangles vertically. You'll soon notice a pinwheel and kaleidoscope look in the quilting project.
- When you apply these pieces over the background fabric, this will complete your quilt top. You can size up and down accordingly.

10. Crazy Quilt: Embrace the freedom of irregular shapes and embellishments in a crazy quilt project.

Crazy Quilt is all about stacking a volume of disparate fabrics in weird shapes together. This Picasso-looking quilt gives you the freedom to patch where you like. Here's how you can make one yourself:

Instructions

- This is a time of absurd applique quilt. You need to have all 12 ½" fabrics of different sorts. Use a ruler and outline an absurd shape. Cut the first fabric at an absurd angle or shape. Ensure, to not cut square or any other shape.
- Now, take a background fabric and stitch the shape over with ¼ inch seam allowance. Iron after each application.
- Add 4-5 long strips with 2 ½ width around all the sides of that absurd shape. Ensure not to use excessively long strips.
- Now, keep repeating this step of layering around the layers with strips. Pin and stitch at the same time. When you reach your goal size of the quilt, you'll be done.

These were some advanced designs that required more tension and attention. Now, it's time to completely game up. Move on to the next section for some expert-level quilting projects.

QUILTING ADVANCED PROJECTS

1. Mariner's Compass Quilt: Tackle the intricacies of piecing together a Mariner's Compass, a complex and compass-inspired design.

Here is a step-by-step guide to help you get a Mariners Compass quilt.

Instructions

- Use a pattern for this quilt to cut exact shapes. This will speed up your process and make things easier for you. Cut the curved triangles accordingly. You can cut four fabrics at once.
- Cut four triangles with 6-inch length and 2 ½ inch width. Then, cut four more triangles with 6-inch height but 1 ½ inch width. Now, cut eight more triangles with a 4-inch height.
- Cut a 14x14-inch circle from a colourful fabric. Take another 16x16 inch white coloured fabric and draw a 14x14 circle on it. Cut the white circle from between. Now stitch the colorful circle in that white square.
- Now, from the 16x16 circle that you discarded cut an 8x8 circle. Stitch it in the middle of the coloured circle that you've just sewn. Take the eight triangles and start stitching them at the gap of two inches.
- Cut a small circle with a 4x4 circle and stitch a bit in the middle of the 8x8 circle. Stitch the 6-inch and 2 ½" four triangles around the circle. Then, for the remaining 1 ½" triangles, stitch them within the gap of the firstly stitched triangles.
- You can apply this pattern too.

2. New York Beauty Quilt: Challenge yourself with foundation paper piecing and curved seams in this traditional yet intricate pattern.

This can be a bit tricky than the previous tutorial. However, if you use a template cutter things can get eventually easier for you.

Instructions

- Get a square of the background fabric of about 9". Then, get 5 navy prints with 2.5"x1.5" measurement. Cut eight pink strips with measurements 5"x1.5". Then, you need grey print cut into 9 pieces with 5"x2" and 4 strips with 2.5"x2". Lastly, one square of 3x3 from yellow fabric.
- Get the pattern printed on paper. Just as learned in the "Advanced Techniques" chapter to trace the pattern from the back side and cut accurately. Also, learn the placement from there. This helps when you don't want to invest in templates.
- Stitch all the triangles appropriately by following the printed design.
- Finish off by placing a circle in between. This design is similar to the previous tutorial.

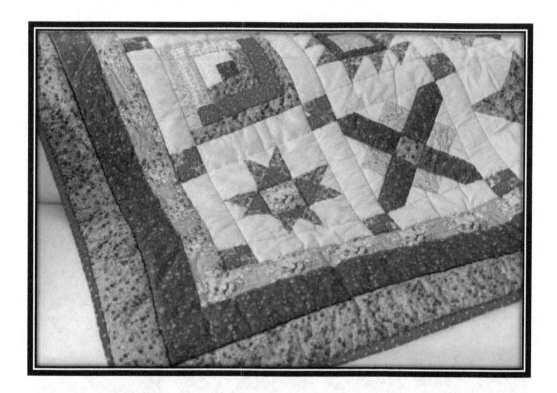

3. Lone Star Quilt: Create a Lone Star pattern with precise angles and intricate details.

Making a lone star requires you to work with a plethora of fabrics. Move downwards to learn more.

Instructions

- Take five different printed fabrics. Cut them all 42 inches long with 1- ½ inch width. Cut 5 strips. Number them, 1,2,3,4, and5. Also, now choose the most prominent fabric and cut one more strip from it. For instance, take 2 as an example.
- Now cut them all half in length. You'll have 12 strips now. Now, make three sets of the fabrics. Here will be the placement ((1,2,3), (2,3,4), (3,4,5)). The strips will be aligned with this template. Now, layer the strips in the set side-by-side but at a distance of ½ inch length-wise.
- The poles should look like network signals. Now, place the ruler at 45 degrees over the poles and cut diagonally. Keep cutting the poles at a distance of ½ inches. Repeat for all sets.
- Now, stitch the three diamonds from each cut horizontally. However, they'll be placed vertically. Take this set of three diamonds from all sets. Position them next to each other side-by-side. You'd notice a bigger diamond. Repeat the process until you make eight bigger diamonds.
- Stitch the first four side-by-side. Repeat for the remaining four. Then, stitch both patches from the center. Add fabric to the background. Your quilt is ready!

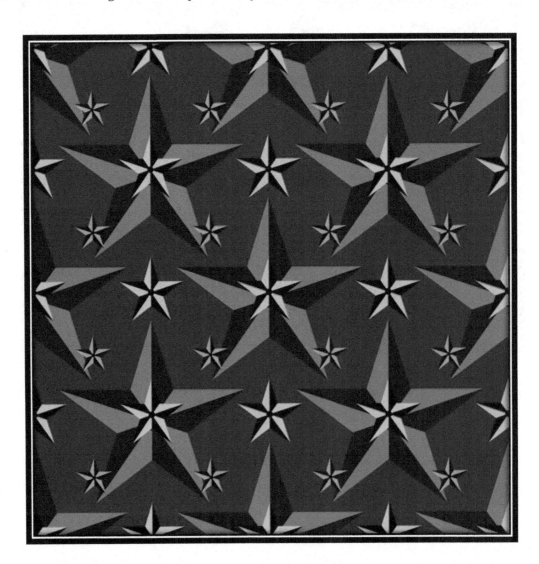

4. Double Wedding Ring Variation: Explore variations of the classic Double Wedding Ring pattern, incorporating unique elements.

You may follow the instructions given in the previous chapter. Use different fabrics and prints to make multiple rings with different styles. Then, you can assemble them to create a variegated look for your quilt.

5. Millefiori Quilt: Inspired by millefiori glass, create a quilt with intricate, multicoloured designs.

It is a kind of hexagon pattern. It involves doing patchwork inside the shape. Here are a few instructions to help you get there.

Instructions

- This is gonna be a bigger quilt with multiple patterns. So, brace yourself. Get 428 pieces of 5-pointed stars with 1¼" measurements. Also, cut 206 pieces of 10-pointed stars, 1368 pieces of isosceles triangle, and 640 pentagons of the same size.
- Get acrylic templates for easier cutting.
- Plant a hexagon in between all the shapes.
- You can decorate the rest of the quilt with the given shapes and pieces. This will result in multi-colored and vibrant quilt.

6. Paper-Pieced Landscape Quilt: Use foundation paper piecing techniques to depict a detailed landscape in your quilt.

Making this quilt can be easier for you if you print out the design. Otherwise, you can also outline the design on the paper. Mostly, the paper-pieced landscape design consists of many fabrics. Their layers are joined to create a landscape view.

Instruction

- Choose a template or take inspiration from Pinterest. Now, draw or print out the design you like. Cut your fabric strips according to the chosen template.
- It is an easier way to design the quilt pattern.

7. Cathedral Window Quilt: Master the art of creating three-dimensional, folded fabric windows for a stunning effect.

This is comparatively not as hard a quilt pattern as the others. Follow the instructions below to get an accurate cathedral window.

Instructions

- Get a solid fabric and cut a 7" square out of it. Also, get vibrant and colorful fabric and cut 2" squares. Turn the edges a bit and press them.
- Stitch the 7" square in half by stitching the sides. This will create an open pocket. Turn it right side out.
- Lay it flat with edges making it look like a triangle. Stitch the center too. Iron over the cloth to let it lay flat.
- Now, turn the four edges and stitch them in the middle. Stitch two squares together horizontally forming a line.
- Take the 2" square out that you cut in the beginning. Change its direction to a triangle and place it between the joining ends of stitched squares. Place it there and turn the edges giving a curtain view to your piece. Pin the setting and stitch it to get the cathedral window. Keep on repeating the process until you cover your desired quilt shape.

8. Curved Log Cabin Quilt: Challenge your skills by incorporating curves into the traditional log cabin block.

Curved log cabin can be easy for you to make if you've already made the log cabin pattern. Here are some instructions to help you get the right curved log cabin pattern.

Instructions

- Follow the same instructions as given for the log cabin design. However, ensure to make four pieces to create this curved piece.
- However, the only tip for this one is to keep the logs at the top points light-coloured. Also, for other logs, use a bright or deep colour. So, the curved log cabins show in the quilting pattern.

9. Art Quilt with Thread Painting: Combine quilting and thread painting to create a detailed and textured art quilt.

This quilt is more about machine stitching. Here's how you can get an art quilt with thread painting.

Instructions

- Get a printable fabric. Get all the threads matching all sides of the printed picture.
- Start stitching with the thread around the corner of the icons in the pictures. Outline and shade them as needed.

10. Intricate Hexagon Quilt: Explore hexagon-based designs, combining precise piecing and intricate patterns.

This intricate hexagon quilt consists of mini 3" hexagons stitched side-by-side. Here's what you need to do!

Instructions

- Take different colored fabric. Iron the fabric before you start stitching.
- We recommend you take cardstocks of hexagon shape. Cut the squares 4x4. Wrap them around a 3" hexagon covering it. The additional 1 inch will be turned and stitched later.
- Now, turn the hexagons upside down over the wrong side. Turn all edges over each other and start stitching by passing the needle.
- Make a lot of them and press along with the making. Stitch the hexagons in rows and stitch the rows together later. Continue making until they cover the desired quilt size.
- Remove the cardstocks and happy quilting!

This is all about interesting shapes, designs, and patterns. Jump down to the next chapter to learn about some common facts and queries regarding quilting!

FREQUENTLY ASKED QUESTIONS

What is the most important thing in quilting?

Accuracy is the most crucial part of successful quilting. This means keeping the fabric from fraying over the edges. Also, keeping the corners clean and cutting accurate shapes. The ripped-out threads and uneven seams are a big "NO" in quilting.

What type of batting should be used?

It is recommended not to use older batting. Also, don't go for battings that are available at lower rates wrapped in plastic. They don't make a good filling for the quilts. I recommend using Quilters Dream Cotton and Hobbs 80/20.

Which fabric is best for making a rag quilt?

To be honest, it solely depends upon the volume and weight of denim. However, it is always better to choose flannel as backing. The visuals just get better. You can only use denim if it is extremely low weight. You may skip the middle layer.

What is a Long arm Quilting machine?

Quilting is usually the process of moving all layers of the quilt below the needle of the sewing machine. However, in a long arm quilting machine, the machine's needle and head move while the fabric remains intact. It keeps the layers from losing their position. Its head is capable of rotating in all directions such as forward, side-by-side, and backward respectively. It is capable of stitching 36 square feet in one go.

Which type of quilting should I choose?

Usually, it is recommended to go for edge-by-edge quilting. The thing is that the quilts are used to do heavy-duty work. Mostly, the quilt patterns are very busy. Hence, it is essential to stitch in such a way that the threads don't fray. Other than that, you can custom quilt too.

What is Custom Quilting?

This type of quilting is done to make signature quilts such as heirlooms. They often have specific intricate signs, sayings, texts, blocks, patterns, and different levels of creativity. In custom quilting, different fabrics and threads can be used at specific places for identification. The piece can highlight a specific patchwork or work of blocks. It can be anything.

To make a rag quilt do you have to use flannel fabrics?

Cotton is a fabric that ravels well if you want to make a rag quilt. However, you can say that flannel is a more traditional option because it is super soft. Consequently, the frays are fluffier and bouncier too. However, it is always a good choice to use at least one layer of plain flannel fabric to upgrade the quilt's look.

Any Quilting tip?

Adding mechanical or sewing machine oil on the shaft of the scissors makes your quilting experience effortless.

What to consider while choosing the batting to be used?

Here are a few things to keep in your mind:

- What is the purpose?
- Will it be washed frequently?
- Do you want it to be soft or sturdy? Determine puffiness.
- Colour of the backing and top layer
- Natural fibre

How to make quilting easy?

Always iron as you quilt the fabric to smoothen the fabric. Use templates if the shape is too hard. Do not stress yourself out. Also, you can get printouts and outline the shape to cut the accurate patterns.

CONCLUSIONS

Quilting is a fun activity. It has room for creativity, innovative input, and intrusive ideas. There is no correct approach to making the quilts. Once you master the basic shapes, you can put them together according to your taste. The great thing is that there are hard and fast rules. You can the fabric type, quilt size, and colors of your choice. It becomes more challenging yet entertaining as you continue doing the work. The work can be hard but it is worth the wait.

In this book, we have detailed the whole outer and inner view to make a quilt. From shrinking and washing fabric to flattening the fabric layer-wise, you get it all. We have also dedicated a few special chapters for adding sashing, cornering, and appliqueing techniques. They are a bonus to make your quilting journey more vibrant.

At the end of the book, we've given you some homework. Make sure to try most of the quilting projects yourself. Don't forget to give us feedback about which one was the hardest. We'd be more than happy to see your work. Happy Quilting!

YOUR EXCLUSIVE BONUS

Scan the QR-CODE below to get your exclusive bonus!

Made in the USA
Las Vegas, NV
12 December 2024

14039809R00050